THE
of LANDSCAPES
SURREY

GRAHAM COLLYER

– *Photographs by* –

DEREK FORSS

COUNTRYSIDE BOOKS

NEWBURY, BERKSHIRE

Countryside Books
3 Catherine Road
Newbury, Berkshire

To view our complete range of books,
please visit us at
www.countrysidebooks.co.uk

ISBN 1 85306 713 X

Produced through MRM Associates Ltd., Reading
Printed in Italy

CONTENTS

Ockley

FOREWORD

A county of many contrasts, that's Surrey. A mixture of urban streets and motorways, of countryside and pretty villages.

It has adapted to the requirements of 21st century living, and thus there is a sense that the Surrey to be found in the writings of Eric Parker and Gertrude Jekyll one hundred years ago has largely been consigned to history.

However, if you stray off the beaten track in an attempt to discover the real Surrey, you will find there is a treasure chest of interest and antiquity. It is an area of many delights.

Divided from west to east by the chalk spine of the North Downs, crossed by a number of lazy, meandering rivers and punctuated by hills such as Hindhead, Leith, Pitch and Holmbury, Surrey has many miles of open country and some wonderful, far-reaching views.

Derek Forss has been taking pictures of Surrey landscapes for many years and, using a mixture of film and digital photography, this book is a perfect demonstration of the natural beauty that still remains.

Getting away from the pace of modern life is possible, and featured on the following pages are some of the places that make up this fascinating county, so much of which is protected by the green belt or owned by the National Trust.

Chaldon

A WALK ACROSS THE COUNTY

'Tis distance lends enchantment to the view,
And robes the mountain in its azure hue.
Thomas Campbell, *Pleasures of Hope* (1799)

Less than one-third of the North Downs Way is in Surrey, but the walk from Farnham to Tatsfield affords some of the most spectacular views of the county. The length of the Way through Surrey is 45 miles, and it is a further 108 miles to Dover.

Since ancient times there has been a trackway running along the ridge of the North Downs. Medieval walkers on their pilgrimage from Winchester to Canterbury would have mainly used tracks at the base of the Downs, later named the Pilgrim's Way and often confused with the North Downs Way, though in places they do overlap.

The long distance path was officially opened in 1978 and, although it makes an unpromising start beside the busy bypass at Farnham, it soon moves away from the noise and fumes of the traffic and enters delightful woodland to pass Moor Park where Jonathan Swift (1667-1754) wrote *Tale of a Tub* in 1704. At Puttenham are the last hop fields in Surrey, and in Compton the Watts Gallery commemorates the life of the great Victorian artist George Frederic Watts, who lived nearby.

After the River Wey is crossed at St Catherine's just outside Guildford, where a bridge replaced a ferry many years ago, the path soon starts to climb to St Martha's Hill. The church here was documented in 1200 and rebuilt in 1850, although there is a tradition that in AD 600 pagan Saxons martyred Christians on the hill in an attempt to halt the spread of Christianity.

Buckland Hills on the North Downs Way

The western part of Surrey is now behind us, and as the height is maintained the remainder of Surrey unfolds via Newlands Corner, Hackhurst Down, Ranmore, Box Hill, Reigate Hill, Tandridge Hill and on to the county boundary.

The 'temple' on Colley Hill is a North Downs Way landmark

Thousands are collected from the idle and the extravagant for seeing dogs, horses, men and monkeys perform feats of activity, and in some places, for the privilege only of seeing one another.
Soame Jenyns (1704-87), *Thoughts on the National Debt*

Much of the village centre at Lingfield is a conservation area and around the church of St Peter & St Paul are a number of fine timber-framed houses. The Pound, or the Cage, is a curiosity now, but it was an important part of the village a century and more ago. It was effectively the jail, or lock-up, and was used as such from the time it was built in 1773 until 1882. A celebrated break-out occurred in 1850 when eleven poachers took advantage of a dozing guard and, with the help of friends who removed the roof, made good their escape.

Older still are the Cross, dating from 1473, which originally marked the boundary between two manors, and the large hollow oak tree beside the Pound, which is believed to be more than 400 years old.

However, to see a tree that may be the oldest in Surrey a journey two miles north of Lingfield is worth making. In the churchyard at Crowhurst is a hollow yew that one estimate puts at 4,000 years old and another at half that, but whatever its age the yew is certainly venerable and one of the treasures of the county.

Horse-racing at Lingfield Park is more than 100 years old and offers sport and betting for National Hunt and Flat enthusiasts. An all-weather track has brought a new dimension to the venue in recent times.

Haxted Mill

To the north-east, Haxted Mill on the River Eden can be traced to 1580. Its working life ended in 1945 and a museum was opened in 1969. Although the Eden is thought of as a Kent river, it does rise in Surrey, just south of Oxted, but soon after Haxted flows over the border and on through Edenbridge.

The Pound beside the old oak tree at Lingfield

THE TUNNEL BENEATH THE DOWNS

If we see the light at the end of the tunnel,
It's the light of the oncoming train.
Robert Lowell, *Since 1939*

When the London to East Grinstead railway opened in 1884 the developers moved in and the area round Limpsfield and Woldingham began to change in appearance. The manor of Limpsfield belonged to Battle Abbey from the time of Domesday until the 16th century, although only the church and courthouse have survived as buildings put up by the abbey. Fortunately, there are a number of medieval buildings still standing in the High Street, which is a conservation area.

The church of St Peter is in a prominent position in the centre of the village, and buried in the churchyard is the composer Frederick Delius.

The National Trust owns much of the open space about Limpsfield, and the High Chart close to the border with Kent is popular with walkers who use the network of footpaths and bridleways. The Greensand Way, a 105-mile path that runs from Haslemere to near Ashford in Kent, crosses Limpsfield Common and the High Chart.

To the north of Limpsfield, and beyond the M25, is Woldingham, which is high up on the North Downs. Marden Park, now a school in the valley beside the railway lines, is a reminder that much of the area was once part of the Marden Estate.

Battles over the railway have loomed large in the history of the area, even as recently as the 1970s when the Government

South Hawke near Woldingham, where the railway passes through a tunnel under the North Downs

planned to build a terminus at Marden Park as part of the Channel Tunnel link. Much earlier, in 1836, talk of driving a railway through the local countryside was resisted and this spirit continued into the Victorian age until the promoters of the iron road got their way, albeit by having to build a long tunnel under Woldingham.

The church at Limpsfield Chart

MOTORWAYS ARE HERE TO STAY

The rolling English drunkard made the rolling English road.
A reeling road, a rolling road, that rambles round the shire . . .
G. K. Chesterton, _The Rolling English Road_ (1914)

It may be difficult to believe, but it has been said that there are more miles of motorway in Surrey than in any other county. Since the M1 was constructed 40 years ago, so much of the country has been ripped up in the pursuit of enabling traffic to get from here to there more quickly. Towns and villages, for so long blighted by heavy traffic rumbling through their centres, are supposed to be better off. In fact, neither aim is wholly achieved, as too often motorways become gridlocked and drivers resort to other routes in an effort to keep moving.

Surrey's own spaghetti junction is at Merstham where the M25 and the M23 meet. The M25, London's orbital motorway, is probably the most infamous road in the country. Always busy, often blocked by accidents, it is shunned by many drivers, who prefer, instead, to take the 'old' roads, thus leaving villages such as Bletchingley and Godstone with a feeling of helplessness. It runs through the county from east of Limpsfield to close to the perimeter of Heathrow airport.

The M23 is the southern extension of the A23 London to Brighton road, starting just north of Merstham and crossing into West Sussex at the entrance to Gatwick airport. Surrey's third motorway is the M3 that starts at Staines near the boundary with Greater London, runs south-west and crosses into Hampshire at Frimley. These are three arteries that in the last three decades have irretrievably changed the face of Surrey.

Bletchingley

It is the towns and villages on the A25 that have most felt the effects of the coming of the motorway. Apart from Bletchingley and Godstone, Redhill and Reigate and Dorking and Abinger Hammer all continue to feel the weight of traffic rumbling past their front doors in a way that the road planners never considered. So much for progress.

Multi-level transport, the M25 and M23 at Merstham

THE WINDMILL AT OUTWOOD

_I had rather live with cheese and garlic in a windmill, far,
than feed on cakes and have him talk to me in any
summer-house in Christendom._
William Shakespeare, _Henry IV, Part 1_

Just over 40 years ago there were two mills at Outwood, but in November 1960 the smock mill collapsed. Now the post mill remains to draw visitors to this village to the east of the M23. The mill is said to be the oldest one still working in the country, and men building it for Thomas Budgen, a miller from nearby Nutfield, are reputed to have been able to see the Great Fire of London.

In 1790 a smock mill was built a few yards away following an argument between two brothers to 'take the wind out of the other's sails'. Ironically, it was Mother Nature rather than any human destructive force that led to the younger mill being blown down in a gale.

Outwood Post Mill draws visitors to a part of Surrey that has seen its fair share of change brought on by the growth of Gatwick airport and the even closer motorway. The countryside south of Reigate has been changed for ever by the development not only of the airport but also of the town of Crawley, which is also just over the border in West Sussex.

Seven hundred years earlier, the old market town of Reigate welcomed a group of Augustinian monks who founded a priory there. After the dissolution it was turned into a mansion by Lord Howard, whose son was one of our naval heroes, along with Drake and Raleigh, against the Spanish Armada. The Georgian

Reigate Park

building, which is now a school, replaced the Tudor mansion and incorporates a little of the original priory, but it is the extensive public park that is the legacy of the Augustinian order.

The twin towns of Reigate and Redhill have always been important trading posts in the east of the county and, until the construction of the M25, were badly affected by traffic on the A25. Even today, with the motorway often the slower option, motorists continue to use the route through the towns.

The post mill at Outwood

THE PLAYGROUND OF LONDONERS

Box Hill must be pretty nearly the best known hill in the world.
Eric Parker, *Highways and Byways in Surrey,* 1908

The great chalk escarpment of Box Hill rises to 563 feet above the River Mole and there are wide ranging views across the Weald to the South Downs. The North Downs Way and the Pilgrim's Way cross it and its downland turf has always attracted crowds of visitors. Box Hill was the playground of Londoners who were brought out of the capital in charabancs long before the motor car ruled the A24 that winds its way around the foot of the hill. The trees that gave the hill its name are still very much in evidence at what is undoubtedly Surrey's best known landmark.

For two centuries the story of Major Peter Labilliere has amused visitors. He moved to Dorking after retiring from the Marines and was known as a harmless eccentric. He spent long periods in meditation on Box Hill and every year would travel to stay with his friend the Duke of Devonshire. In 1799 his visit was extended to three months and when he returned to Dorking he told his landlady that he would die in nine months. He was as good as his word, and having obtained permission to be buried on Box Hill he left instructions that his coffin should be placed upside down.

The story goes that the major believed that when the world at last turned topsy-turvy he would be the right way up. But there is a different theory, apparently borne out by his diaries, and that is that as an admirer and follower of St Peter he wished to follow the apostle, who was crucified on an inverted cross, and be buried the wrong way up.

The Pilgrim's Way on Box Hill

Box Hill, which was given to the nation in 1914, was where the idea of television began to become a reality, for its inventor, John Logie Baird, was a tenant of the prominently placed Swiss Cottage in the early part of the last century.

The zig-zag road at Box Hill

Please to remember the Fifth of November,
Gunpowder Treason and Plot.
We know no reason why gunpowder treason
Should ever be forgot.
Anon

When the time comes around each year to remember, remember the fifth of November, thoughts will turn to Brockham, the little village in the Mole Valley under the chalk escarpment of Box Hill. Here is held Surrey's biggest commemoration of Guy Fawkes's attempt to blow up Parliament, the bonfire and fireworks display attracting 10,000 and more people on a cold, dark night.

Only at Chiddingfold is the size of the crowd rivalled, but all over the county, and usually on the first Saturday in November, fires blaze and rockets woosh into the night sky in this traditional event that marks a time in our history that probably could not be recounted with any accuracy by most of the people who turn out to watch.

Of course, the best time to visit Brockham is in daylight and when the sun is shining. The village green and old cottages are a delight, and it is little wonder that Brockham has caught the eye of the judges in the county's best kept village competition through the years.

The village got its name because of the badgers that frequented the area, but nowadays you are more likely to catch a glimpse of a kingfisher skimming across the River Mole as you are of secretive old brock.

Cottages at Brockham

Badgers and cars do not see eye to eye, and it is a sad fact that the closest most people get to a badger is a dead one. Badger setts are protected by law, but that does not stop these fascinating creatures being persecuted by criminal elements, which is why the work of the conservation groups is so important.

Picturesque Brockham Green

LINKS WITH QUEEN VICTORIA

When we build, let us think that we build for ever.
John Ruskin, *Seven Lamps of Architecture* (1849)

Lord Ashcombe is buried in the churchyard at St Barnabas on Ranmore where the church that he built in 1858 is a local landmark. His former house, Denbies, now gives its name to the vineyard on the sloping countryside hereabout that produces England's best known wines.

Ashcombe was a prominent landowner across the county, whose father, Thomas Cubitt, had started out as a carpenter and, when he died in 1854, left £1 million made from a life in the building trade in London. His son George inherited the fortune and was ennobled as the first Lord Ashcombe in 1892.

Cubitt did much to develop Victorian London and a great deal of his work remains, including parts of the front of Buckingham Palace, and buildings in Belgravia, Bloomsbury and Pimlico. He was the son of a Norfolk farmer who worked as a ship's carpenter, but he was clearly a man ahead of his time. He worked hard to stop London becoming enveloped in smoke from domestic and industrial chimneys, and also had clear thoughts on improving the capital's drainage problems.

His work found favour with Queen Victoria and he was engaged to build Osborne House on the Isle of Wight, the monarch's favourite residence. Subsequently, it became a talking point when, having bought the Denbies estate in the 1840s, he rebuilt the mansion in a style so reminiscent of Osborne House. He even had to deny that Denbies was to be a royal hunting lodge for the Prince of Wales. Thousands of trees and rare specimens from Kew Gardens were planted in the grounds, but he was unable to enjoy the fruits of his labours for too many years because he died at the age of 68.

Ranmore from Logmore Lane

A winter day on Ranmore

THE RIVER THROUGH THE DOWNS

All in its midday gold and glimmering
See, through the trees, a little river go.
John Keats, *Endymion* (1818)

Surrey's second river is 42 miles long from its source in West Sussex to the Thames at Hampton Court. Meandering through meadows and occasionally disappearing from view, the Mole cuts its way through the chalk of the North Downs.

The river is probably best known in the Mole Gap where it is crossed by stepping stones that convey walkers on their way up Box Hill. The stones first appeared in 1932, the gift of the then Home Secretary, James Chuter Ede, who had attended school locally, and were declared open by none other than Clement Attlee, the Prime Minister, who had family connections with the area. However, those early stones were unable to withstand the erosion caused by the current, and were replaced 14 years later by more robust blocks.

Downstream at Burford Bridge there is a more conventional crossing and here the eponymous hotel has always been a stopping off point for travellers, so much so that in 1908 Eric Parker considered it to be a 'sort of Swindon of the Dorking Road'. Nelson spent the night there, and bade farewell to Lady Hamilton, before going off to do battle at Trafalgar. And in 1818, Keats, while staying at the hotel, found the trees and the peace of Box Hill just the right environment to enable him to finish *Endymion*.

From Burford Bridge the river follows a path to Leatherhead and then wanders off through fields to become

The Mole at Burford Bridge

visible from the M25 motorway, which crosses it twice. The Wey is close here, but the two rivers then drift apart, the Mole to turn to the north on its final leg to the Thames.

Stepping stones across the River Mole

GRAND HOUSES AND THEIR SETTINGS

Won't you come into the garden?
I would like my roses to see you.
Richard Brinsley Sheridan, *To a young lady*

Among the great houses of Surrey, two stand out and attract large numbers of visitors. The National Trust owns both and of the two, Polesden Lacey is the better known.

Set on the North Downs near Great Bookham, the Anglo-Irish playwright Richard Brinsley Sheridan (1751-1816) had a mansion there before the present house was built for £7,600 in 1824 by Thomas Cubitt (*see* Ranmore), for Joseph Bonsor, a successful City stationer and bookseller. Cubitt had yet to buy nearby Denbies but he had fallen in love with the Surrey Hills, something generations of builders and developers have done in the subsequent century and a half.

The building was extensively remodelled in 1906-09 by the Hon Mrs Ronald Greville, a well-known Edwardian hostess, whose collections of paintings, furniture, porcelain and silver are displayed in the reception rooms and galleries, as they were at the time of her celebrated house parties. Mrs Greville gave the property to the National Trust in 1942, and it and the extensive grounds, a walled rose garden, lawns and landscape walks have been enjoyed by the public ever since.

The Duke and Duchess of York, who were later to become King George VI and Queen Elizabeth, spent part of their honeymoon at Polesden Lacey in 1923.

Hatchlands at East Clandon was built in 1758 for a naval hero, Admiral Edward Boscawen, and although his death came

Hatchlands at East Clandon

only three years later he was able to give the architect Robert Adam his first commission in England. Hatchlands has been owned by the Trust since 1947 and its present tenant is Alec Cobbe, a picture restorer and collector who has the world's largest number of keyboard instruments on display. A small garden by Gertrude Jekyll is seen at its best from late May to early July.

Polesden Lacey

GARDENS KNOWN AROUND THE WORLD

All gardening is landscape painting.
Alexander Pope

There are many picturesque and interesting gardens in the county that open to the public, but by far the most famous is the Royal Horticultural Society's 60 acres at Wisley.

The original garden was the creation of George Ferguson Wilson, who was a businessman, scientist, inventor and keen gardener and a former treasurer of the RHS. He bought the site in 1878 and established an experimental garden with the idea of making 'difficult plants grow successfully'. The garden acquired a reputation for its collections of lilies, gentians, Japanese irises, primulas and water plants.

On the death of Wilson in 1902, the property was sold to a wealthy Quaker, Sir Thomas Hanbury, who had already developed the garden at La Mortola on the Italian Riviera. The following year, Hanbury donated Wisley to the society, which soon moved its garden from Chiswick, which it had leased since 1822.

A mile or two up the A3 at Cobham is Painshill Park, one of Europe's finest 18th century landscape gardens and contemporary with Stourhead and Stowe. It was created by the Hon Charles Hamilton, plantsman, painter and designer, between 1738 and 1773 when he transformed barren heathland into ornamental pleasure grounds and parkland of dramatic beauty and contrasting scenery, dominated by a 14-acre lake fed from the River Mole by a waterwheel.

For almost two centuries the gardens were well

Splendour recreated at Painshill Park

maintained, but after the Second World War they became derelict and 20 years ago were in a sorry state. This is when the Painshill Park Trust was formed and over the last two decades it has restored 160 acres of the grounds to their original splendour. There IS now a variety of habitats for visitors to enjoy, plus the society has planted three types of vine in an attempt to reproduce the sparkling wine for which Hamilton became celebrated.

A gardener's delight at Wisley

A TOWN OF GASTRONOMIC DELIGHT

Here is wine,
Alive with sparkes – never, I aver,
Since Ariadne was a vintager,
So cool a purple.
John Keats, *Endymion* (1818)

South Street, Dorking

Britain's largest vineyard is near Dorking and in less than two decades Denbies wine has established itself in the marketplace. But there is nothing new about producing wine on the slopes of Ranmore where the 265-acre estate is situated, for the Romans also grew vines there.

Dorking has a reputation for food and drink. Eric Parker said its 'real' history has traditions of the table and the cellar. The Romans also brought poultry to the area and the true local fowl has five toes, and is depicted in the town's crest. *The Gentleman's Magazine* in 1763 observed that 'an incredible quantity of poultry is sold in Dorking'.

It was also famous for a fish dish called water-souchy, the fish having been caught on the Sussex coast, and in the Surrey Archaeological Collections is the following recipe of 1833 'by a Lady': Stew two or three flounders, some parsley roots and leaves, 30 peppercorns, and a quart of water, till the fish are boiled to pieces; pulp them through a sieve. Set over the fire the pulped fish, the liquor that boiled them, some perch, tench or flounders, and some fresh roots or leaves of parsley; simmer all till done enough, then serve in a deep dish. Slices of bread and butter are to be sent to the table to eat with the souchy.

A gentlemen's club used to meet in the Red Lion to discuss the tench and flounders, and large white snails found on Box Hill were a delicacy. A wild cherry produced red wine that was said to be a little inferior to French claret but would keep longer.

All in all, a town of gastronomic delight.

Dorking from Denbies vineyard

A TREASURE AMID THE PINES

The three great elements of modern civilisation,
Gunpowder, Printing and the Protestant religion.
Thomas Carlyle (1838)

The hamlet of Friday Street is one of Surrey's treasures. Tucked away amid the pine woods to the north of Leith Hill, it is an area beloved of walkers and riders. Its tranquillity is its greatest asset, but the number of visitors it attracts so often shatters this peace. They come because of its beauty, and the sense it gives of being cut off from the outside world.

It is not difficult to imagine what it was like back through the centuries. The pond is thought to have been there at the time of the Domesday survey, although it makes no specific mention. However, there were several mills listed in the Wotton Hundred and Friday Street's hammer pond is quite likely to have been associated with one of them.

Corn would have been ground there in those days, but by the time of Henry VIII there was a powder mill in the isolated valley that was reckoned to be the first of its kind in the country.

A quaint letter box from the reign of Edward VII, at the northern end of Friday Street, is a reminder that time does not move very fast in these parts. Beyond it runs a footpath beside the infant Tillingbourne as it carves its way through the Wotton Estate where carpets of bluebells and the emerald green of newly leafed beech trees are such a delight in the spring.

When you take a westerly route out of Friday Street you soon arrive at Abinger Common where St James's is second only

Pines on Abinger Common

to Coldharbour's as the highest old parish church in the county. The oldest parts are late 11th century, the most recent addition being an organ to mark the millennium. It replaced a temporary one brought into service more than half a century earlier when a German flying bomb struck the church and knocked out the original instrument.

Reflections at Friday Street

UP, UP AND AWAY

And did those feet in ancient time
Walk upon England's mountain green?
William Blake – *Jerusalem*

Winter scene at Coldharbour

Coldharbour is Surrey's second highest village and one of the most popular. It is criss-crossed by footpaths and bridleways, and nestles on the slopes of Leith Hill.

The Plough has long been a hostelry where weary travellers slake their thirst and after recharging their batteries they can reach the summit of Leith Hill by taking a track opposite the pub. Climbing steadily through woodland, and past the cricket ground, the occasional clearing offers wonderful views across a vast expanse of the Weald to the South Downs.

The ancient Britons who lived here in the hilltop fort known as Anstiebury Camp would have known these views. The ten-acre site was a refuge for Iron Age women and children while the menfolk were away fighting. The boundary ditches are still discernible today.

One winter's abnormal rainfall recently gave Coldharbour a problem it neither courted nor expected. When a landslip opened up a chasm in a road, it not only closed an important artery for local residents and visitors alike, but raised questions about the stability of the surrounding hillside. It was even suggested that Leith Hill was on the move, although there were reassurances that the landmark tower was safe.

The road through Coldharbour

LEITH HILL AND ITS TOWER

When I am living in the Midlands
That are sodden and unkind . . .
And the great hills of the South Country
Come back into my mind
Hilaire Belloc, *The South Country* (1910)

Leith Hill, the highest point in the county and in the whole of the South East, commanded, said John Aubrey in the 17th century, views of the whole of Surrey and Sussex. Also to be seen were parts of Hampshire, Berkshire, Buckinghamshire, Oxfordshire, Hertfordshire, Middlesex, Essex and Kent, not to mention, with the aid of a telescope, Wiltshire, plus 41 of London's church spires.

Trees now make the vista less all embracing, but there is still a spectacular canvas to be enjoyed. Towns and villages are dotted over the countryside far below, and with a little imagination you can bring to mind what Aubrey saw, until perhaps the intrusive sound of a mobile phone will snap you out of your reverie and dump you back into the 21st century.

Whichever way you approach the 965 foot summit you are faced with a long haul up winding steps and narrow gulleys. The tower built in 1766 is tall enough to bring the overall height to a mountainous 1,000 feet above sea level. It was erected by Richard Hull of Leith Place, and when he died six years later he was buried at its foot.

Hull furnished two rooms in the tower but after his death it fell into ruin. Many of the blocks of stone were removed and eventually it was part-filled with cement and left as a curiosity for

Leith Hill Place

half a century. Then, in 1862, Mr Evelyn, the Lord of the Manor, decided to again make it available to the public but found the concrete too hard to be broken and so built a new staircase in an attached tower.

Leith Hill Place itself is situated below the hill and much of the countryside around it is owned by the National Trust. In spring the carpets of bluebells are a gorgeous sight and there are also rhododendron glades and some fine old trees.

Leith Hill Tower

THE DEATH OF A BISHOP

By me you know how fast to go.
Motto on the clock at Abinger Hammer

Close by Abinger Hammer is a memorial that records the accidental death in 1873 of Samuel Wilberforce, the Bishop of Winchester, who was thrown as his galloping horse stumbled in a rabbit hole. The bishop was the son of William Wilberforce, the great anti-slavery campaigner, but he was also well known in his own right.

He was a notable critic of Charles Darwin and, in 1860, while Bishop of Oxford and the vice president of the British Association for the Advancement of Science, he addressed 700 people, many of them fellow Anglican clergy, and tore to shreds Darwin's recently published book, *The Origin of Species by Means of Natural Selection.* Darwin, who was very ill and unable to attend, was represented by his leading supporter, Thomas Huxley.

Wilberforce had gained the nickname 'Soapy Sam' from his days as a student at Oxford, where he exercised a certain degree of slipperiness in ecclesiastical arguments, and on that day in June 1860 his powerful oratory and measured debate engaged him in an almighty spat with Huxley. It was the talk of Victorian dinner parties and there are many historians who have suggested that it might well have been the defining moment in the great debate on science versus religion in the 19th century.

The simple memorial, with the bishop's initials, pastoral staff and date of death carved into the granite, is at Abinger Roughs. In Abinger Hammer itself, the Tillingbourne-fed

Familiar scene at Abinger Hammer

watercress beds were once hammer ponds used by Surrey's ironmasters. Those industrial days are remembered by the village's famous clock, whose blacksmith figure stands proud above the A25.

Hackhurst Downs from Abinger Roughs

WALKING THE GREENSAND WAY

This is heaven's gate.
Mrs G.E. Street on arriving in Holmbury St Mary in 1872

Like the North Downs Way, the Greensand Way is primarily for walkers, and there are only a few sections of bridleway open for cyclists and riders. It extends for more than 55 miles across Surrey from Haslemere to Limpsfield Chart on the Kent border, and follows the Greensand ridge across the southern half of the county. Five north-south links connect it with the North Downs Way.

The late Geoffrey Hollis and other local ramblers, with the support of the Surrey Society and Surrey Voluntary Service Council, devised the route. A 12-mile pilot scheme crossed Leith Hill, the county's highest point, and was officially opened in 1980 to celebrate Footpath Heritage Year. Geoffrey Hollis was well-known as the compiler of walks published in the county newspaper, the *Surrey Advertiser*.

In many respects the Greensand Way provides more interesting and varied walking than the North Downs Way. It may not maintain the height of the more northerly route, but there are places where the walker will be made to puff a bit – Pitch, Holmbury and Leith hills, for example. John Aubrey reckoned Holmbury Hill was a mountain but at 875 feet its top is lower than both Leith Hill and Gibbet Hill at Hindhead. In the Stone Age, Holmbury Hill was topped by a camp of 500 people, among whom were potters whose work has been dug up and deposited in the museum at Guildford.

Cricket at Holmbury St Mary

In more recent times, stone was dug on the hill and used to build the church at Holmbury St Mary to the design of George Edmund Street (1824-81), the celebrated architect of the Law Courts in London. When Mr and Mrs Street first saw the village in 1872 its name was Felday, but after he had built a house and called it Holmdale, and then planned and paid for the church, the present name was adopted.

Holmbury Hill

THE RIVER THAMES

The Thames is liquid history.
John Burns, British Liberal politician to an American who had compared the Thames disparagingly with the Mississippi.

The greatest of our rivers flows through the northern part of the county, but unlike the Wey and the Mole there is not the same sense of belonging. Both run into the Thames, at Weybridge and Hampton Court respectively, while ol' man river rolls gently on to the sea.

The river enters the county from Berkshire at Englefield Green and close to the Magna Carta memorial. Until Egham it

separates the two counties, but from there it is wholly in Surrey until it reaches West Molesey. Here the river keeps Surrey apart from Greater London, but when Long Ditton is reached the county turns its back on the Thames.

The development of Chertsey was originally due to its status as an island, surrounded by marsh, the Thames and its tributaries. A monastery was established in AD 666 and survived two pillages to become the wealthiest religious house in Surrey. The monks were responsible for the establishment of the town in the 12th century, and it became the centre for trade in the area.

Agriculture and market gardening brought prosperity, as well as the manufacture of bricks and tiles up until the last century. However, as with so many other towns, the coming of the railway proved to be the start of a period of boom. The station was built in 1848 and very soon the town began to expand.

Chertsey Bridge

The River Thames at Laleham

No free man shall be taken or imprisoned or dispossessed, or outlawed or exiled, or in any way destroyed . . . except by the lawful judgment of his peers or by the law of the land.
Magna Carta, Clause 39

Churchyard at Thorpe

As we approach the 800th anniversary of the signing of the Magna Carta, the meadows beside the Thames at Egham will increasingly become the focus of world attention. King John's historic signature on 15th June 1215, proclaimed freedom and liberty for the people, and from that day the lives of our ancestors were said to have been different. In truth, it probably strengthened the hand of the monarchy, but over time Magna Carta has come to symbolise something very important in our way of life, even in our psyche.

The meadows were used as a racecourse from the 18th century until 1886 and, with Windsor nearby, attracted royal patronage. They were given to the National Trust in 1931, and the site is marked by the work of two great architects with strong Surrey connections. Sir Edwin Lutyens, who was born in Thursley and whose distinctive work can be found all over the county, designed kiosks and lodges, while a memorial by Sir Edward Maufe, the architect of Guildford Cathedral, was unveiled in 1957. It was commissioned by the American Bar Association and paid for by contributions from 9,000 of its members.

Four years earlier Maufe had designed the Air Forces Memorial on neighbouring Cooper's Hill which records the names of 20,456 airmen with no known graves who lost their lives in the Second World War, over Britain and Northern and Western Europe.

Also close by is a memorial unveiled by the Queen in 1965 to the memory of President John F. Kennedy of the United States, who was assassinated on 22nd November 1963. The inscription records that 'this acre of English ground was given to the United States by the people of Britain in memory of John F. Kennedy ...'

Few, though, discover the tiny village of Thorpe, once a notable farming community whose 14th century church of St Mary and village hall and pub from the 17th and 18th centuries are delightful reminders of times past.

The Magna Carta memorial at Runnymede

A ROMAN BUILDING, A LAKE AND A TOTEM POLE

And under the totem poles – the ancient terror –
Between the enormous fluted Ionic columns
There seeps from heavily jowled or hawk-like foreign faces
The guttural sorrow of the refugees.
Louis MacNeice, *The British Museum Reading Room* (1941)

Virginia Water, like Box Hill, acts as a magnet for visitors who stream out of the suburbs to smell the country air. The construction of the 120-acre lake was undertaken in the 18th century under the direction of the Duke of Cumberland. In 1746 he had vanquished Bonnie Prince Charlie and his band of Scottish warriors in a bloody battle at Culloden near Inverness. Cumberland became known as the Butcher of Culloden, but subsequently took on the title of Ranger of Windsor Park.

His collaborator in the scheme to drain the marshy acres of the southern end of the park was his deputy Thomas Sandby, who was a Royal Academician and landscape gardener. He decided that a lake would be a suitable way in which to rid the land of excess water, so he dammed a number of small streams with the result that two and a half centuries later his early drainage scheme gives enjoyment and pleasure to tens of thousands of people every year.

To the west of the lake are the remains of a fine Roman building recovered from Leptis Magna near Tripoli in North Africa. They were brought to England and presented to the Prince Regent in 1816. There was a suggestion that they be used for the portico of the British Museum, but this did not materialise and they were established at Virginia Water in 1826.

Totem pole at Virginia Water

Children and the not so young are always fascinated by the 100 foot high totem pole at Virginia Water that was erected in 1958 to mark the centenary of the founding of British Columbia.

The exclusive Wentworth estate, built on Surrey heathland where the secluded homes of millionaires from the world of commerce, sport and showbusiness are set amid the pines, is known to golfers the world over because of its three courses – the East and West which were laid out in 1924, and the Edinburgh which was opened by Prince Philip in 1990.

Virginia Water

LOWLAND HEATH AT ITS BEST

People will not look forward to posterity, who never look backward to their ancestors.
Edmund Burke, 1790

Chobham Common is one of the largest areas of heathland in Surrey, and is valuable both as an amenity and as an area of outstanding wildlife interest. It has been recognised as one of the finest examples of lowland heath in Europe, and in 1994 was designated a national nature reserve.

Lowland heath is a globally rare and unique habitat supporting a variety of specialised plants and animals. West Surrey was covered by heathland two centuries ago, but now less than one-fifth remains. It is a precious resource and the Surrey Heathland Project is responsible for carrying out large-scale practical management using machinery and grazing animals and, of course, volunteers. And by promoting its work, the organisation is making more people aware of the importance of retaining a habitat that our ancestors took for granted.

Unless you read the inscription on the memorial on Chobham Common you might never realise how important this tract of Surrey heathland was in the defence of the country. The granite cross records the day Queen Victoria reviewed her troops, who were encamped on the common almost a century and a half ago. It was erected in 1901 as the parishioners' memorial to the late monarch and captures the summer's day on 21st June 1853, when the queen travelled to the ridge to inspect 8,129 of her troops who were on manoeuvres.

As a result of what she saw a decision was taken to give the

Queen Victoria memorial on Chobham Common

army a permanent home, and with all speed Aldershot was chosen to be the place. Whether this signalled the death knell of much of the beauty of West Surrey, as one commentator observed in the 1930s, is open to debate, but one thing is certain, the army, whose home continues to be Aldershot, has made a great difference to the area.

Gorse and heathland on Chobham Common

BROOKWOOD CEMETERY AND MEMORIES OF WAR

The cemetery is an open space among the ruins,
Covered in winter with violets and daisies. It might
Make one in love with death, to think that one should
Be buried in so sweet a place.
Percy Bysshe Shelley, *Adonais* (1821)

When 2,000 acres of heathland on the outskirts of Woking were bought in the mid-19th century it was the start of what was to become one of the largest cemeteries in the country. The Necropolis Company of London required an Act of Parliament to open a burial ground for London's dead in 1854, and soon funeral trains were to be a daily occurrence on a dedicated railway line from Westminster to Brookwood. Initially, one-fifth of the acreage was laid out as a last resting place, and the wealthy and celebrated were buried side by side with the capital's ordinary folk.

Thirty-five years after the cemetery was opened, a crematorium was built, and in 1917 land was set aside for the burial of Commonwealth and American service personnel who had lost their lives in the London area during the First World War. There was a further extension required for the dead of the second great conflict.

Brookwood Cemetery is known throughout the world and receives a constant stream of visitors. Its two parts are in stark contrast: the civilian burial ground is a rambling somewhat dishevelled area where at almost every turn the visitor can be confronted by the unexpected and the unannounced. In the military section it is, as you would expect, as neat as a new pin with row upon symmetrical row of headstones.

The Basingstoke Canal

The 37 acres make Brookwood the largest war cemetery in the United Kingdom, and there are some imposing memorials, including the Brookwood Memorial, a large circular structure on which there are the names of 3,500 men and women of the Commonwealth and Empire forces who were posted as missing, presumed dead, in the Second World War, and for whom there are no known graves.

The Basingstoke Canal passes through Brookwood on its 37-mile journey from Greywell in Hampshire to the Wey at Weybridge. It was opened in 1796 and 32 miles have been restored for recreational use. There are 28 locks on its 15 miles through Surrey, during which it falls 195 feet.

Brookwood Cemetery

AN AGATHA CHRISTIE MYSTERY

There runs a road by Merrow Down,
A grassy track today it is,
An hour out of Guildford Town
Above the River Wey it is.
Rudyard Kipling

The church of St Martha-on-the-Hill

Ask a stranger what they know of Surrey, and Newlands Corner will possibly be high on the list. Agatha Christie aficionados will be able to tell you about the time that she staged her own mystery there by disappearing for several days and setting off a national police hunt.

By any stretch of the imagination it is a fine area of countryside with wide, open views and good walks. Most visitors, though, rarely leave the car park and congregate close to their vehicles or the cafeteria and ice cream van, so if you stride out along the North Downs Way or any of the other paths you can usually find peace and solitude.

From Newlands Corner there is so much to see in no distance at all. The downs of Merrow and Pewley will take you to Guildford, the villages of the Tillingbourne valley are close by, so too is the Silent Pool where, according to legend, King John saw a woodcutter's daughter swimming naked. The frightened girl drowned, along with her brother as he attempted to rescue her, and her ghost haunts the pond to this day.

The North Downs Way will take you to the hilltop church of St Martha from where you can turn on to the Downs Link path and head for the South Downs. This route bridges the gap between the North Downs Way at St Martha's Hill and the South Downs Way at Steyning in West Sussex. Much of the 30 miles follows the track of the Guildford to Horsham railway, which became a victim of Beeching in the 1960s.

The original railway was built in two sections: the first in 1861 went north from Shoreham, and the second south from Guildford to Christ's Hospital at Horsham in 1865. One hundred years on and the axe fell, a decision that seems crass today as the area between Guildford and Cranleigh continues to grow and suffers as a result of the increased volume of motorised traffic.

Newlands Corner looking towards the South Downs

A MAGNET FOR VISITORS

. . those scenes made me a painter and I am grateful.
John Constable, 1821

If Surrey has a 'chocolate box' village it is surely Shere, and its beauty causes it to be overrun by vehicles. When a bypass was constructed to the north of the village in the 1960s it did bring relief from the constant battering the old buildings were taking, but decades later the time has come to take another look at traffic movement before the very essence of Shere is destroyed for ever.

Artists and writers have always been attracted to the village by its scale and harmony, and one house was, at different times, the home of three Royal Academicians. Modern day painters, both professional and amateur, are drawn by Shere's charm, and they jostle for space with the walkers, the pubgoers and the visitors.

If you have time to visit the church of St James in the centre of the village, you will find peace away from the madding crowd. Here worshipped William Bray who, in 1801, aged 65, picked up the pen of the late Owen Manning, one-time vicar of Peper Harow, and visited every church and parish in the county in order to complete the important *History of Surrey*, a magnificent work much used by researchers down the years.

The White Horse pub in the centre of the village is a magnet for visitors. In 1908, Eric Parker said it was the only inn in Surrey known to him that sold a guide to the neighbourhood. Now, there is a leaflet or a guide on just about every one of the county's attractions, and tourism in Surrey is a major industry.

Old bridge at Shere

St James's church at Shere

A FAMOUS ARCHITECT LEFT HIS MARK

But a house is much more to my mind than a tree,
And for groves, O! a good grove of chimneys for me.
Charles Morris, *Country and Town* (1840)

Work by Augustus Welby Northmore Pugin, the foremost architect and designer of the 19th century, is to be found in three places in Surrey, but by far the best known examples are the tall chimneys in the centre of the village of Albury, set in the Tillingbourne Valley under the North Downs.

Pugin (1812-1852), whose most famous work is probably the Houses of Parliament, also designed the Drummond Mortuary Chapel in Albury Park for the lord of the manor, the banker Henry Drummond, as a memorial to the lives of his three sons, Henry (16), Malcolm (21) and Arthur (20), who died in the years from 1827 to 1843. The chapel forms part of the 1,000-year-old church in Albury Park and is also the last resting place of Drummond, his wife Henrietta and their daughter Adelaide, who was 65 when she died.

Pugin's other work in the county is at Peper Harow, near Godalming, where the church of St Nicholas and the gatehouse and barn at Oxenford can easily be overlooked. In 1842, four years after his engagement with Drummond, the architect began work on the gatehouse and barn, which can be seen from the B3100 Milford to Elstead road. The coat of arms of Lord Midleton of Peper Harow is carved on the inner boss and an ox crossing a ford, which gives the place its name, is depicted on the outer boss.

Two years later Pugin began work on St Nicholas' church for Lord Midleton who asked him to create a Norman chancel

Waterloo Pond in the Tillingbourne Valley

arch. Given his preference for Gothic architecture he was not keen to do this, and made his point by including Gothic arches in the left aisle.

There are a number of ponds in this part of the Tillingbourne Valley, some of which were associated with the manufacture of gunpowder at Chilworth from as early as the 16th century.

The old church in Albury Park

MESSING ABOUT ON THE RIVER

I often wished that I had clear,
For life, six hundred pounds a year,
A handsome house to lodge a friend,
A river at my garden's end . . .
Jonathan Swift, _Imitation of Horace_ (1714)

Travelling by boat in Surrey has been commonplace since Charles II was on the throne. Acts of Parliament led to the county's principal river, the Wey, being made navigable, and transport by barge continued until well into the last century. Now, pleasure craft make their stately progress between Godalming and Weybridge and offer an entirely different view of the landscape.

Sir Richard Weston, who inherited Sutton Place near Guildford in 1613, was the first person to see the possibility of canalising the Wey. He thought a system of waterways he had seen in Holland might be suitable and set out to prove it. He and then his son built 12 locks and 10 miles of canal for £15,000 and thus began the process of revolutionising the movement of goods.

The cut was extended the four miles from Guildford to Godalming in 1764, and just before the end of the 18th century the navigation was linked to the Basingstoke Canal, to be followed 20 years on by a union with the Wey and Arun Canal at Shalford.

The National Trust centre at Dapdune Wharf in Guildford faithfully records the working life of the navigation, and among the celebrated vessels built there was _Reliance_, which traded between Guildford and London Docks until she was holed and sunk in a collision with Cannon Street Bridge in 1968. Ignominiously towed to Leigh-on-Sea, and further damaged by

Shalford Mill

vandals, _Reliance_ was discovered by the National Trust in 1989, refloated and towed back home to be restored.

Shalford Mill situated on the Tillingbourne, at a point just before it reaches the Wey, is another National Trust treasure. In the late 1920s it became the headquarters of 'Ferguson's Gang', the identity of whose members remained a mystery as they campaigned to preserve the English countryside. They supported the National Trust and eventually handed over the Mill to its safe-keeping.

Narrow boat on the Wey Navigation at Shalford

GUILDFORD: THE COUNTY TOWN

Guildford is a beautiful city, let us keep it that way.
Eric Parker

If ever a townscape needed no introduction it must be Guildford High Street. It is breathtaking, although all too often it is overrun by vehicles, scaffolding and builders' materials. Steep and cobbled (granite setts to be precise) and framed by buildings dating back to medieval times, the scene is completed by the Guildhall and its clock which overhangs the street. It is a picture that has been taken to all the corners of the earth by the overseas visitors who are drawn to the county town (not yet a city in spite of Eric Parker's claim).

Guildford nestles in the Wey Valley in a gap in the North Downs. The golden ford that gave the town its name was believed to have crossed the Wey somewhere close to the foot of the High Street. The ford, of course, has long gone and now, several bridges later, the river through the town centre is barely given a second glance by the crowds who pack Guildford in search of some of the best shops outside of the West End and the ever-growing nightlife.

What was once a market town, and the centre of a productive agricultural area, is now the base for large companies whose business is new technology. Complementing this trend is the University of Surrey, which is one of the leading technological seats of learning in the country. Even the Anglican cathedral is 20th century and the most recent to be built in this country.

Guildford Cathedral of the Holy Spirit

Guildford, then, is a town of contrasts whose history spans the last millennium but whose future depends, to a large extent, on the continued growth of service industries and new ideas.

The River Wey close to Guildford town centre

Lord Finchley tried to mend the Electric Light
Himself. It struck him dead: And serve him right!
It is the business of the wealthy man
To give employment to the artisan
Hilaire Belloc, *More Peers* (1911)

The Pepperpot in Godalming High Street

The claim of Godalming to have been the first town in the world to have its streets lit by electric light makes Godhelmians feel justly proud. In 1881 a generator at the leather mill at Westbrook in the town produced enough power to enable the mayor and corporation to disconnect the gas supply that had until then illuminated the street lights. There is a celebrated illustration depicting the old town hall, the landmark Pepperpot in the High Street, all lit up. So history was made. Even though three years later gas was again being used, the stage was set for the world to take up Godalming's pioneering spirit.

The town has always been important because of its position on the rivers Wey and Ock, from whose waters mills were operated from Domesday times. Cloth was manufactured there from the 13th century and 300 years later the newly invented framework knitting machine made the town an important centre for hosiery manufacture.

Godalming remains a country town, with its Lammas Land beside the Wey preventing it from being over-developed, but the nature of the countryside around about has changed and there are far fewer farms. It is not a market town any more. Many farms have been transformed into country estates with large houses behind electronic gates, which epitomises the area as what has become known as the 'stockbroker belt'. The rich and famous choose to live in the Godalming hinterland, and many send their sons and daughters to Charterhouse, one of the country's leading schools, which moved out of London to Godalming in 1872.

The world famous gardener Gertrude Jekyll lived at Munstead, just south of the town, and her designs, coupled with the architecture of Sir Edwin Lutyens, with whom she collaborated, are prevalent here. Nearby is the National Trust's Winkworth Arboretum, breathtaking beauty on a hillside running down to two lakes.

Narrow boats on the Wey Navigation at Godalming

THE FOLD COUNTRY

My fire is out, my forge decayed,
And in the dust my vice is laid,
My coal is spent, my iron gone,
My nail is drove, my work is done.
Epitaph on the Chiddingfold gravestone of Arthur Stedman,
18th century blacksmith

The villages in the Fold Country, Chiddingfold and Dunsfold among them, are as old as any in Surrey. Tucked away in the south-west corner of the county, they are now very much the sought-after location of the wealthy incomers who populate the rural areas in large numbers. It was not always thus, of course, for these villages were once some of the most deprived and isolated in Surrey, and home to rural folk who maintained little or no contact with the outside world.

Chiddingfold's village green is its focal point. The old forge, where Arthur Stedman would have worked, is still in use, and it has been overlooked by some of its neighbouring buildings, including the Crown Inn, for more than 500 years.

Visitors to the church will be drawn to a lancet window in the west wall, the glass of which was made in the village. Chiddingfold was the centre of a great glass-making industry, and it has been claimed that before the 16th century most of the glass made in England originated from the furnaces in this corner of Surrey. One Lawrence the Glassmaker of Chiddingfold made white and coloured glass for Westminster Abbey more than 700 years ago.

Every November, Chiddingfold's bonfire night draws

Chiddingfold

thousands of people who gather on the green for an annual celebration that began in the 19th century. It is a good natured evening, but in 1929, after the build-up to the event had got out of hand, the chief constable sent 250 police officers to the village, and a Justice of the Peace threatened to read the Riot Act.

The yew tree in the churchyard at Dunsfold, whose age has been put at certainly 1,000 years and probably double that, overshadows all of Chiddingfold's antiquity. Surrey's venerable yews are all delightful, but those at Dunsfold and Crowhurst are by far the most celebrated.

Hascombe Hill, on the edge of the Fold Country

COMMON GROUND AND QUIET PONDS

Four ducks on a pond,
A grass-bank beyond,
A blue sky of spring,
White clouds on the wing:
What a little thing
To remember for years –
To remember with tears!
William Allingham (Irish poet and husband of Surrey artist
Helen Allingham), *A Memory* (1888)

The many commons between the Hog's Back and Hindhead are
favourite places for walkers and riders. They are similar in so
many ways, but they all have their individual characters – and

Warren Pond, one of the six at Cutt Mill

names: Bagmoor, Crooksbury, Guinea, Hankley, Ockley,
Puttenham, Royal, Thursley. Considering their proximity to the
A3 and A31 roads, they are still places where you can escape. They
are not wild in the moorland sense, but they have a character all
of their own. They are sandy and heathy, packed with wonderful
flora and fauna, and great for birdwatching.

The villages of Puttenham and Elstead are good starting
points to explore these open spaces. Before leaving Puttenham,
take a look at the church on which, until a fire in 1736, there was
a spire, and walk past the pretty cottages in the main street. The
common stretches away to the south-west, criss-crossed by a
number of paths that can lead you to the secluded ponds at Cutt
Mill.

The Tarn, the second of the six, is the pond that is open to
the public and frequented by anglers. A causeway that carries the
road from Puttenham to Elstead separates it from Cutt Mill Pond.
At the opposite end of the Tarn is an excellent view of Warren
Pond, and beyond that are Long, Trout and General's ponds.

The mill at Elstead was probably one of the six in the
Farnham Hundred at the time of the Domesday survey, and the
church dates to 1138. From the village the land rises gradually the
further south you go, and once on to Thursley Common there is
a sense that you are approaching the climb to Hindhead. Of all
the commons in this part of the county, this one is by far the most
important, and Thursley Bog is a site of special scientific interest.
Here, too, you can spot the reclusive Dartford warbler as it skips
from one gorse bush to another.

Puttenham Common, south of the Hog's Back

THE GREAT CHALK SPINE

There is no other road on which you can walk so far and see so much broad Surrey country open out . . .
Eric Parker, *Highways and Byways In Surrey,* 1908

The North Downs split Surrey from west to east and the section between Farnham and Guildford is known as the Hog's Back. Motorists, unfortunately, have turned it into a racetrack, and the northern spur road through the Blackwater Valley, which follows the county border with Hampshire and was completed in 1996, has increased the volume of traffic.

Some of the most stunning views in Surrey can be had from the Hog's Back, although drivers are advised to keep their eyes on the road. To the north and north-east, the vast panorama stretches away into Berkshire, Buckinghamshire and to the capital, where the London Eye and the landmarks of the City and Docklands can be seen. To the south and south-west, are the heights of Hindhead, its higher West Sussex neighbour, Blackdown, and the South Downs, which block out the view of the Channel. And to the west, the once great Hampshire forest of Alice Holt and the fertile Wey Valley take the eye towards Alton and Winchester.

Seale is a picturesque village on the southern side of the Hog's Back, but for history make for Wanborough, just to the north of the ridge, where Romano-British remains have yielded many important finds. The monks at Waverley Abbey from the 12th century tilled the farm with its great, and now restored, barn, and the 13th century church is on the site of a Domesday building.

The church of St Lawrence, Seale

Two centuries ago Morris Birkbeck, a Quaker, was the tenant farmer until he set sail for the United States and founded a community in Illinois which he named, not unnaturally, Wanborough. Letters home attracted the interest of many of his former employees, including the brothers Edward and James Collyer, from Elstead, who set sail from Liverpool in April 1818. Two more brothers followed four years later, and today, with the aid of the internet, this writer has constructed a branch of his family tree he did not know existed.

Trees and meadows viewed from the Hog's Back

THE MONKS OF WAVERLEY

. . . for the love of Christ's Passion . . . help the preservation of this poor monastery.
The abbot to Thomas Cromwell at the Dissolution

The great abbey at Waverley was the first Cistercian house in the country, but has been in ruins since the Dissolution in 1536. The path to the ruins is through meadows in front of Waverley Abbey House and its lake, and there is a fine example of one of the many bridges in the locality that were built by the monks of Waverley.

The abbey ruins are a joy simply to wander through, trying to imagine what daily life must have been like for the generations of monks who knew it as their home in the 400 years of its existence.

Nearby is one of the county's curiosities: Mother Ludlam's Cave. Named after the so-called white witch of Waverley, it has also been known as St Mary's Well and, by William Cobbett, Mother Ludlam's Hole. A cave was first mentioned in the Waverley Annals where it was stated that the abbey's water supply ran dry in 1216 and the well was called Lud(e)well. A monk named Brother Simon found an alternative source at what became known as St Mary's Well from which he laid lead pipes to carry water to the abbey.

Cobbett was disappointed when he showed his son Mother Ludlam's Hole in the 1820s. 'Alas it was not the enchanting place that I knew . . . The semi-circular paling is gone; the basins, to catch the never ceasing little stream, are gone; the iron cups, fastened by chains, for people to drink out of, are gone; the pavement all broken into pieces; the seats for people to sit on, on

Ruins of Waverley Abbey

both sides of the cave, torn up and gone; the stream that ran down a clear paved channel now making a dirty gutter.'

Now, its state is best described as neglected but the tales of Mother Ludlam, the friendly witch, continue to be handed down through local families, and linked to the great cauldron in the parish church at Frensham.

Bridge built by the monks at Waverley Abbey

FROM COMMON TO CRICKET

Far finer cricket's to be seen,
Down where I live on Tilford Green.
There we can play for cricket's sake . . .
By a player who often appeared in first-class matches.
Farnham Herald, 1951

Hankley Common stretches away to Elstead and on towards Thursley. It is an area of mixed use: golf, walking, riding and military. Soldiers have trained on Hankley since the 19th century, and the mock sea wall built as part of the preparations for the Second World War D-Day landings in France can still be seen near to the natural bowl known as the Lion's Mouth.

If there is any village in Surrey that is quintessentially English it is Tilford, one mile to the north. Compact around a triangular green on which cricket has been played for two centuries, Tilford is one of those places that draws people as if by a magnet. The scene has changed little over the great span of years since the Waverley monks built the east and west bridges. Here, the two branches of the River Wey merge and flow on as one towards the Thames. When the monks were at the abbey nearby, Tilford was heathy waste but, as farmers, they needed to cross the river and 800 years on their engineering skills are taken for granted.

What the monks did, of course, was open up the heathland, and over time it began to take on a different look as builders moved in. Fortunately, development was controlled and today's Tilford is the result.

The west bridge at Tilford

The Barley Mow public house and its adjoining cottages have looked out on the green for centuries, and when William 'Silver Billy' Beldham, the greatest of the early Hambledon and England cricketers, retired to run the pub in 1822 his view would have been of animals grazing on the green, and the little chapel in front of Church Farm.

The church had not yet been built, nor the school, and it was many years before Lutyens was invited to design the Institute and decided to use the stones from the by now redundant chapel. These buildings now make up the picturesque scene at Tilford.

Hankley Common

THE RICH HISTORY OF FARNHAM

Rock of Ages, cleft for me,
Let me hide myself in Thee . . .
The Rev Augustus Montague Toplady, born in Farnham in 1740

Church Lane, Farnham

The great park above Farnham was once full of deer and the scene of royal hunts. It is even thought Henry VIII may have hunted there, a belief strengthened a few years ago by the discovery in the park of a Tudor hat pin, a find about which mystery was to continue when it was stolen in a daring raid on Farnham Museum.

If the king did hunt in Farnham Park he would have stayed in the castle next door. Farnham Castle and Castle Street below it dominate the old market town and from its keep, now owned by English Heritage, there are excellent views across the surrounding countryside.

The history of the castle, which has a Norman tower, is rich and often bloody. Civil War battles between the Parliamentarians and the Roundheads made Farnham a key town. Later, successive Bishops of Winchester lived there and now it is a centre for international briefing that brings visitors from many corners of the world to the area.

Farnham is a bustling town whose status as an important livestock and beer-making centre has long passed. Hop fields to the east and west were prominent as recently as 1960, but the Maltings, which is now the arts centre, ceased to be used for the production of beer several generations ago. Farnham United Breweries gave secure employment to many in the town until well into the last century, but the writing was on the wall when the pattern of brewing began to change and in time the conglomerates took over. Little wonder then that the Farnham beer festival has for more than 20 years been a successful event with the nation's real ale enthusiasts.

The parish church has a prominent position in the town centre and its churchyard is the resting place of William Cobbett, Farnham's most famous son. Its most celebrated sporting son, the motor racing ace Mike Hawthorn, who won the world championship title in 1958 shortly before he was killed in a road crash at Guildford, is buried in the cemetery on the outskirts of the town.

Avenue of trees in Farnham Park

THE BISHOP'S FISH

Fish say, they have their stream and pond;
But is there anything beyond?
Rupert Brooke, *Heaven* (1915)

The two ponds at Frensham act as a magnet for visitors. The Great Pond, beside the A287 Farnham to Hindhead road, is the more popular; the Little Pond on the other side of King's Ridge beloved of walkers. Both stretches of water are havens for wildlife and a birdwatcher's paradise.

The origins of the ponds date back to the 13th century when the Bishop of Winchester, then resident in Farnham Castle, had them constructed as a means of supplying fish for his table. The Great Pond was certainly known in 1208 and was enlarged from a natural spring-fed pool. The Little Pond followed 38 years later.

Over the centuries the ponds, together with a third called Abbot's Pond at Tilford, whose dam broke in 1841 and was not replaced, produced untold quantities of fish for the bishops. In the last century, though, there were many changes, and now Frensham ponds are owned by the National Trust and managed by Waverley Borough Council. Walkers and riders are provided with a variety of marked trails, and at times the countryside can get overrun with visitors.

However, it is still possible to get a sense of the Frensham Common of the past by standing on King's Ridge, with its barrows, and looking down on to both ponds. This would have been a superb vantage point in 1913 to watch the first seaplane trials on the Great Pond. Months later, though, the heathland

St Mary's church at Frensham

below the ridge had been transformed into a vast transit camp as the soldiers of the First World War waited to be sent off to the front. So many did not return, and their final memory of England was not of their home town or village but of a bleak and, in those days, rather featureless Surrey common.

In the lovely old church of St Mary is the giant cauldron associated with Mother Ludlam of Waverley (see page 68).

Tranquil setting of Frensham Great Pond

HINDHEAD AND ITS GRISLY PAST

The most villainous spot God ever made.
William Cobbett, *Rural Rides* (1822)

In September 1786 the name of Hindhead became widely known because of a dastardly murder committed high up on the slopes of Butterwedge. The villains were soon caught and, after trial, were returned to the place of their crime and hoisted on a gibbet, where their bodies swung in the wind until, as skeletons, they were brought crashing down in a thunderstorm more than three years later. The murder of the so-called 'unknown sailor' has intrigued generations of folk ever since and the name Butterwedge soon disappeared from all but the earliest maps, to be replaced by Gibbet Hill.

It commands views to the north and north-west across much of Surrey and as far as the London Eye and the tallest of the capital's buildings. The Celtic cross is a reminder of the grisly events of the past. It was placed on the site of the gibbet in the middle of the 19th century in an attempt to bring a sense of peace to the area and to rid it of the demons that were still associated with the bleak hillside.

Far below, broom-makers lived in their hovels in the depths of Heccombe Bottom, which was already known as the Devil's Punch Bowl. Hindhead was indeed an inhospitable place, much feared by travellers between London and Portsmouth. The old turnpike road that climbed over Gibbet Hill had been replaced in 1826 by what eventually became the A3 but it remained a difficult journey, and long after the Second World War it was not unusual to see cars come to a halt in a cloud of steam as their radiators boiled dry on the slow ascent.

Celtic cross that marks the site of the gibbet at Hindhead

Nowadays it is more likely to be drivers who reach boiling point as they stop-start their way over the top through one of the South East's notorious traffic bottlenecks. Hindhead remains a name in the news. Since the 1930s when a corridor of land was set aside to take traffic away from the crossroads, it has lived in hope of having a proper bypass. Now, at last, a decision has been taken to tunnel under Gibbet Hill and this brings with it the anticipation of an end to the strangulation of one of the most scenic parts of the county.

The Devil's Punch Bowl

OUR HERITAGE HELD IN TRUST

On Hydon's top there is a cup,
And in that cup there is a drop:
Take up the cup and drink the drop,
And place the cup on Hydon's top.
Anon

You cannot go far in Surrey without coming across a National Trust sign. The organisation administers thousands of acres across the South East of England from its regional offices at Polesden Lacey, near Great Bookham. Grand houses such as Polesden Lacey, stretches of countryside, small cottages at Eashing and Hambledon, and the 13th century bridge across the River Wey at Eashing are all examples of the county's heritage which are in the safe-keeping of the Trust.

The lives of two of the three founders of the organisation are remembered in Surrey. Social reformer Octavia Hill (1838-1912) has a granite seat to her memory on the top of Hydon's Ball, a 593 foot hill to the south of Godalming. And Robert Hunter, a solicitor to the Commons Preservation Society and the General Post Office, who lived in Haslemere, is acknowledged as the man who made the move to save Hindhead Common and the Devil's Punch Bowl for the nation. These areas of countryside were, in 1906, the first to be bought by the National Trust, whose aims in the late 19th century were to save historic houses.

Hindhead was much sought after by developers and but for people such as Hunter, this internationally known part of Surrey would surely have been a wholly different place today. The

Eashing bridge is 13th century

Golden Valley, for instance, was bought by public subscription after Marie Stopes, the contraception pioneer who lived briefly in Hindhead, had successfully bid at auction in Guildford in 1928.

Much of the Trust's land is simply meant to be enjoyed, but on Witley Common the education centre is there to instruct. British and Canadian troops were encamped on the common in the two world wars, and because of this its natural habitat changed markedly through the 20th century. It therefore offers visitors a much wider understanding of the countryside and, more importantly, how it can and must be protected.

Pines on Witley Common

Surrey is a county of contrasts. It is a combination of urban streets and motorways, of countryside and pretty villages. In his evocative photographs Derek Forss seeks to reflect the county in all its moods and seasons. From the rivers of the Thames, the Mole and the Wey to the far-reaching views from Box Hill and the North Downs, his pictures portray many landscapes, full of interest and antiquity. The text by Surrey newspaper man Graham Collyer chronicles the county's history and demonstrates just how much it has to offer today, both to local people and visitors alike.

Derek Forss lives in Surrey and has over 40 years' experience in landscape photography. His work is sponsored by Olympus Cameras and he has contributed to many books and magazines.

Graham Collyer was born near Farnham, attended the town's Grammar School, began his career as a journalist at the age of 16 on the *Farnham Herald* and is now the editor of the *Surrey Times and Advertiser*. He has written extensively about the county and is the author of *The Surrey Village Book*.

Front cover photograph: River Wey at Shalford
Back cover photograph: Leith Hill Place